Original title:
The Universe Is Just One Big Question Mark

Copyright © 2025 Creative Arts Management OÜ
All rights reserved.

Author: Ryan Sterling
ISBN HARDBACK: 978-1-80566-061-3
ISBN PAPERBACK: 978-1-80566-356-0

Whispers of the Unknown

Stars giggle in cosmic delight,
As planets debate in the night.
What's the moon hiding behind her veil?
A secret, perhaps, or just an old tale?

Meteor showers rain down with glee,
Who wrote the rules of gravity?
Comets tailing like they're in a rush,
Maybe they're late for a cosmic hush!

Galaxies in Query

Black holes play peek-a-boo,
Sucking in stars just for a view.
Why do they spin? What's their game?
A dance, a trick, or cosmic fame?

Asteroids gather, a wild parade,
"Is this a race?" they're all amazed.
Swirling dust, a celestial dust-up,
Who's winning this galactic cup?

Everlasting Wonder

Planets whisper their hidden lore,
Counting dreams from an alien shore.
Are we the punchline of a cosmic jest?
Or just the universe's quirky guest?

Saturn chuckles with rings round his waist,
"Catch me if you can, I'm not here to waste!"
While Jupiter's storms giggle in stride,
What's in that red spot? Let's take a ride!

Infinity's Puzzles

Mysterious forces twist and turn,
What's the next riddle that we'll discern?
Planets mock us with their bright allure,
"Do you have the answer?" they're eager and pure!

Nebulas dance in a colorful sprawl,
"Can you guess what we're made of at all?"
Yet in this chaos, we laugh and we ponder,
Because questions without answers only lead to wonder!

The Array of Unfathomable Thoughts

In outer space where thoughts collide,
The stars just wink and take a ride.
With every twinkle, questions rise,
And ponder why the chicken flies.

Is that a comet or a sneeze?
What's up with aliens, if you please?
They zoom by fast and take no names,
Do they play interstellar games?

Orbits of Inquiry

Planets spin like tops, oh dear!
They giggle softly, never fear.
What's under Saturn's fancy rings?
A cosmic cat that tears at strings?

Black holes suck in all the fun,
Did they invite the sun to run?
Galaxies twirl, what a sight!
Are they dancing, day or night?

Celestial Puzzles in the Void

A puzzle box in endless flight,
With clues that dance in pure delight.
Are planets just lost marbles, friend?
Rolling where no edges end?

Meteor showers, oh what joy!
Are they just scattered space toys?
With every crash and cosmic clunk,
Do comets giggle in their funk?

Beyond When and Why

What came first, the star or light?
Or was it just a game of fright?
Galaxies whisper secrets tight,
A cosmic riddle in the night.

Do asteroids ever feel alone?
Do they wish for friends, like a phone?
Nebulas puff in colors bright,
Wondering if they're wrong or right.

Dark Sky Whispers

In the night, a silence hums,
Stars giggle as gravity thumps.
Planets dance with their own flair,
While comets pop like popcorn air.

Black holes wink, they're in on the prank,
While we ponder, lost in the blank.
Galaxies swirl, what do they hide?
Maybe it's just a cosmic slide!

Dancing with Doubts among the Stars

Underneath the cosmic dome,
We trip through space, far from home.
Asteroids roll with a cheeky smile,
While time takes breaks in style.

Nebulas swirl like cotton candy,
Giving all our thoughts a bit of dandy.
Planets spin to their own beat,
Encouraging us to tap our feet!

The Enchanted Abyss of Thought

In the depths of cosmic jest,
Ideas float, but never rest.
Thoughts collide in a playful game,
Who knew pondering could be so lame?

Like black holes eating socks, we lose,
Questions swirl in a funky muse.
Answers giggle, hide and seek,
While curious minds break out in squeaks!

Cosmic Reflections in a Question

Mirror, mirror, who's the best?
Stars reply with a twinkling jest.
Stardust chuckles, "Who's counting, friend?"
As time and space begin to bend.

Galaxies grinning like Cheshire cats,
Spinning yarns of curious spats.
We laugh and sigh, forever chasing,
The riddles of this cosmic pacing!

Starlit Mysteries Await

Above our heads, the stars all giggle,
With winks and quirks, they dance and wiggle.
What lies beyond the twinkling site?
A space cat chasing a comet's flight!

Why does Mars wear that rusty face?
Is it shy or just avoiding space race?
And do black holes eat pizza too?
Or just swirl around in cosmic stew?

Why does the sun think it's so bright?
Does it have a secret to share tonight?
Aliens must be laughing away,
As we ponder and chill in our Milky Way!

A cosmic joke, we all can see,
It's all a riddle, and that's the key.
So raise a toast to questions endless,
In this space they call, the splendid mess!

The Galaxy's Unanswered Riddles

In the depths of space, a funny sight,
Aliens play hide and seek in the night.
But where do they go, can you explain?
A cosmic prank, or just a space game?

Why does Jupiter sport those big storms?
Is it a drama? A cosmic norm?
The moon's got craters, she's a bit pockmarked,
Could it be youthful fun, when it sparked?

Stars are born and then they die,
Do they wish for more, please tell me why?
Is Saturn's ring just a fancy hat?
Or is it hiding where the space mice chat?

What if black holes were just a big sneeze?
A cosmic tickle, or a galactic tease?
The answers float like dust in the air,
But isn't it fun to wonder and dare?

Questions Written in Starlight

In starlight's glow, questions shine bright,
Do comets have tails just for the fright?
Is Neptune really just a blue balloon?
Or does it party with Saturn each noon?

Why does Ursa Major hold the bear tight?
Is it keeping it warm on a chilly night?
What do the stars whisper when we're asleep?
A riddle they keep, a secret they keep!

Galaxies swirling in dizzying dance,
Are they just friends, or in a romance?
Why does Pluto feel a bit left out?
A planet's dream, now full of doubt.

So let's roll on this cosmic quest,
Laughing at riddles, life's little jest.
In the vastness where questions arise,
The fun is in searching for cosmic surprise!

Echoes of Cosmic Wonder

Echoes ring through the skies so wide,
With tones that make even comets glide.
Is it music? A cosmic tune?
Or just stars playing hopscotch at noon?

What do quasars giggle about on high?
When they twinkle, do they mean to fly?
Why does the sun always have the lead?
A brightness contest? You bet, indeed!

Planetary parties, who will attend?
Do the moons get along, or just pretend?
Why's Mercury always in a rush?
Is it late for the solar system's hush?

So ponder these patterns, they're quite amusing,
In the vastness of space, there's no refusing.
With laughter and joy, we search every night,
For answers that twinkle, a pure delight!

Queries Amongst the Celestial Bodies

Stars giggle in the night,
Planets ponder in delight.
Why's Pluto been so cold?
Is it waiting to be told?

Comets dance like silly sprites,
While black holes munch on cosmic bites.
Question marks in every hue,
Wondering what they should do.

Asteroids rock, just passing by,
Orbits wave a cheeky hi!
Are they lost or just too free?
Space has jokes just wait and see.

Aliens giggle from afar,
Searching for that perfect star.
Do they laugh at our small dreams?
The cosmos loves its funny themes.

The Constellation of Uncertainty

Orion's belt, a gripping tale,
Why's he always lost at sail?
Looking for his sword each night,
But it's just out of sight!

Big Dipper's caught in a spin,
Where's his cup? Did it begin?
Drifting stars, they shrug and twinkle,
As questions start to crinkle.

Cassiopeia's throne's a chair,
But why so much empty air?
Is she pondering a riddle?
Or just playing with a fiddle?

Each twinkling light gives a wink,
Galaxies giggle, laugh, and think.
Is there meaning in this fuss?
Or just space having fun with us?

Beyond the Boundless Sky

Flying high in the nighttime glow,
What do shooting stars even know?
Each wish comes with a baffled grin,
Are we winning? Are we kin?

Nebulas swirl in cotton candy,
In colors bold yet far from dandy.
What's a supernova's grand plan?
Just a sparkly dustpan?

The astronauts float, heads in the air,
Do they worry? Do they care?
Survey the galaxy's odd parade,
With questions that never fade.

Planets chuckle over space tea,
Throwing cosmic jokes with glee.
Where's home in this endless sprawl?
Stars all seem to have a ball!

The Astronomical Enigma Unfolds

A black hole yawns, what could it eat?
Caffeinated comets dance on feet.
Does it wonder "Where's my meal?"
Or just anxiously spin its wheel?

Saturn's rings laugh, oh so bright,
Are they just twirling in delight?
Waves of gas in a swirling whirl,
Maybe dancing in a cosmic twirl?

Galaxies spin like a merry-go-round,
Comics sprawled on spacetime ground.
"Is this all? Is there more?" we ask,
Peeking through the endless flask.

The cosmos chuckles at our plight,
Finding sense in the endless night.
Questions float and twirl around,
In the stars, the truth is found!

Starlit Riddles

Stars are winking, what do they know?
Comets dash by with a cheeky glow.
Planets spin tales, all in a swirl,
As we scratch our heads, what a big whirl!

Aliens chuckle from galaxies far,
While we ponder where our dreams are.
Is it a joke or a heavenly play?
Let's toast to questions, hip-hip-hooray!

Celestial Inquiries

Why do black holes wear a dark cape?
Are they hiding secrets or just trying to escape?
Shooting stars laugh at our little schemes,
While we just stare, lost in our dreams.

Does Mars really want to be our friend?
Or just spinning tales that never end?
With quirky queries orbiting round,
We dance with doubts, but truth is never found.

A Dance of Doubts

In the sky, questions pirouette and twirl,
While we grind our teeth, lost in a whirl.
Is time a linear noodle or curly one?
Waiting for answers that never come.

With every tick, the clock starts a jest,
Like cosmic jesters at an endless fest.
We toss up thoughts like confetti in air,
And laugh at the puzzles, a celestial affair.

Echoes of Uncertainty

The moon's cheeky grin leaves us perplexed,
Did it hide the cheese, or just play tricks next?
Meteor showers bring giggles and glee,
While we ask the stars for some clarity.

Black holes might munch on the light so bright,
Or maybe they're just on a cosmic diet?
With every twinkle, we toss up a shrug,
Echoes of questions, like a warm snug hug!

The Cosmos' Riddled Heart

Stars giggle in the night,
Planets dance, what a sight,
Questions tumble from the sky,
Is that a comet, oh my!

Black holes whisper, deep and wide,
Gravity's pull, a cosmic ride,
Why'd the quasar cross the lane?
To get to the other space, plain!

Aliens munch on moon cheese,
Sending signals with such ease,
Are they lost or just confused?
Maybe their GPS is bruised?

Asteroids spin, a funny game,
Each one asks, what's my name?
In this vast and silly theme,
Life's a quirky, endless dream.

Milky Way Queries

In the Milky Way, I ponder,
Why do meteors wander?
Is Earth just a speck, a blip?
On a cosmic, wobbly trip?

Shooting stars, do they wish?
Or just zoom by like a fish?
Galaxies swirl, oh what fun,
As they play tag, on the run!

Comets with tails like a kite,
Making stardust, what a sight,
Do they gossip as they fly?
Or simply just wave goodbye?

Distant worlds with funny names,
All part of these cosmic games,
Is Pluto still part of the crew?
Or off making jokes—who knew?

A Universe of Unsaid Things

Between the stars, secrets hum,
With a chartreuse, wobbly drum,
What's that noise, a cosmic joke?
Or just a star giving a poke?

Gravity giggles, pulls us near,
While comets tumble, full of cheer,
Planets chat in friendly debates,
Over who has the best real estate.

Constellations play hide and seek,
While black holes puff and sneak,
Has anyone seen the lost sock?
Maybe it's stuck on the clock!

Quantum leaps, oh what a trial,
Makes scientists scratch and smile,
In this vastness, bizarre and bright,
Lies a question mark every night.

Cosmic Curiosity Unbound

Little asteroids bump and grind,
Searching for what they can't find,
Do they think they're some wild rock?
Or just hatch jokes, tick-tock!

Saturn's rings spin tales of flair,
Wearing bling in its cool air,
Is it the gem of the night sky?
Or just a fancy, twinkling lie?

Silly stars in constellations,
Share their weird interpretations,
Is that a bear, or just a truck?
Funhouse mirrors built with luck!

Questions linger, bold and bright,
In this cosmic dance, such delight,
What's outside this endless sphere?
Perhaps the punchline—are we near?

Orbiting Thoughts in Zero Gravity

Floating through space, what a delight,
My socks lost in a nebula, out of sight.
Planets spin, but I just drift,
Searching for answers as I misplace my gift.

Galaxies giggle, stars start to tease,
I ponder why pizza doesn't float with ease.
Comets crash parties, making a scene,
While I just wonder what it all could mean.

Gravity's pulling at my funny bone,
Why do aliens never pick up the phone?
As I twirl around in an astrological mess,
All my thoughts just swirl, I must confess.

The cosmos laughs in its glittery dome,
With questions so silly, I could never roam.
But in the vast unknown, I find my cheer,
Floating in joy, sipping cosmic beer.

In the Shadows of Celestial Doubt

Stars wink at me, but do they know,
Life's a puzzle with pieces that don't show?
Dark matter hides its quirky secrets,
While I trip over my own thought regrets.

Constellations whisper tales of old,
Yet I prefer stories not yet told.
Could a black hole be a cosmic joke?
Or just a bad idea that scientists spoke?

Planets align, but am I aligned?
Is there a manual for the confused mind?
Asteroids chuckle as they zoom on by,
And I just ask, can fish in space fly?

Navigating doubts in this starry shroud,
Laughing at thoughts that feel so proud.
Amidst the twinkling, my worries fade,
In the shadowed dance, all doubts are laid.

Eclipsed by Questions

A lunar giggle, a solar sigh,
Behind each eclipse, I can't help but pry.
What are we really doing out here?
Are aliens mocking with cosmic cheer?

That shooting star? Was it just my wish,
Or did I miss a celestial dish?
Gravity's pulling, but my mind's afloat,
Is a star just a dot or a noodle in a boat?

While planets tango in a cosmic twist,
I contemplate the questions I can't resist.
Would time travel help me find my ease,
Or just make it worse, like a cosmic tease?

As shadows dance in the light of the moon,
Answers evade in a playful tune.
Embracing the mystery, I laugh and cheer,
For in doubts and questions, I find my sphere.

The Cosmic Labyrinth of What-Might-Be

In a maze of matter, I lose my way,
Cartwheeling thoughts in a comical play.
Wormholes giggle as I pass them by,
As echoes of questions make me sigh.

Jupiter's frown, Saturn's sly smile,
Each planet's peculiar, adds to my trial.
Asteroids bounce like quirky ideas,
While quarks and quirks dance on my fears.

Could aliens be plotting my next snack?
Or just arguing over who's got the knack?
In a cosmic riddle, I lose my train,
Chasing laughter that drives me insane.

Riding comets with a curious grin,
My mind races on this wild spin.
Finding joy in the mystifying spree,
In this labyrinth of wonders, I'll just be me.

Orbiting Around Wonder

Stars twinkle like winking eyes,
Wondering if we're wise.
Planets dance in cosmic tune,
Asking if we've found a boon.

Aliens may be sipping tea,
While we ponder 'what's the key?'
Asteroids throw a cosmic party,
Who invited that big, fat smarty?

The Mysteries of the Cosmos

Galaxies swirl in a grand ballet,
Do they care what we say?
Shooting stars make wishes fly,
Hoping no one hears them sigh.

Black holes hide their secrets tight,
Like introverts avoiding light.
Crack a joke, they might just smile,
But good luck with that, it takes a while!

Light's Enigma

Photons zoom, they love to race,
Chasing shadows like a game of chase.
But why so fast, we want to know,
Do they have somewhere else to go?

We wave at lights, they wave right back,
But what's their secret, cutie crack?
They sparkle, shimmer, play their part,
A riddle wrapped in a light-filled heart.

Infinite Possibilities Cancelling Certainty

In a cosmos of dreams and schemes,
Reality bursts at the seams.
Every answer just leads to more,
What lies beyond that cosmic door?

Fortune tellers scratch their heads,
While we eat our cosmic breads.
Predicting futures, stumbling near,
Is that a star or just our beer?

Space Between Answers

In the cosmos, we spin round and round,
Searching for truths that are rarely found.
Aliens giggle from their high-flying ships,
While we ponder life through caffeine-infused sips.

Stars wink knowingly, just out of reach,
Like a wise old sage on a faraway beach.
Questions float freely on cosmic winds,
But the cosmos just shrugs; it's all in good spins.

The Infinite Searchlight

We wield our flashlights, but where's the beam?
Chasing dark shadows in a glittering dream.
Why did the comet bring a rubber duck?
To splash in the space puddles—what a peculiar luck!

Galaxies dance like they're at a ball,
Tripping on stardust, they'll always fall.
We shout to black holes; they echo our sighs,
As they gobble our queries and play with our lies.

Beyond the Edge of Certainty

What's just beyond that cosmic curve?
Do they have snacks? Do they swerve?
We scribble equations on napkins so neat,
While asteroids giggle and tap to a beat.

The more we explore, the less that we know,
Like trying to catch a green, glowing glow.
Telescope lenses are strangely askew,
As we ponder "What's out there?" oh, if only we knew!

Planets of Possibility

Around every corner, odd worlds we greet,
With creatures who sing and dance on their feet.
Each galaxy offers a brand new surprise,
As we squint at the skies, searching for pies!

Is there life on a donut-shaped sphere?
Will the aliens join us for breakfast and cheer?
In dimensions unknown, endless jokes will flow,
In this riddle of life, we're all part of the show!

Oceans of Uncertainty

Waves of doubt crash, a slippery floor,
Fish in space swimming, who could ask for more?
Nautical questions bubble to the top,
Is there really a way for this fish to hop?

Diving deep where the jellyfish glow,
Quizzical squids put on quite the show.
Riding currents of thought with a grin,
What treasure awaits if we only begin?

Underwater goggles and cosmic stares,
Seaweed whispers about cosmic affairs.
Each splash a riddle, what's the real score?
Maybe it's just fishy, but I want more!

Navigating doubts with a surfboard sleigh,
Catch a wave of chaos, let it carry away.
In oceans of questions, we swim with delight,
What if the stars are just glitter at night?

Starlit Journeys of Inquiry

Sailing ships through skies of dreams,
With telescopes peering at cosmic beams.
What's on the menu in some far-off place?
Aliens cooking at a galactic pace?

Moonbeams chuckle, a wink in their glow,
As we ask why the stars seem to flow.
Every twinkle is just one more line,
In the sky's script, a playful design.

Gravity giggles, in a pull and a sway,
As I float through fancy, lost in the play.
What's this vortex that swallows our glee?
Maybe it's just hungry for more mystery!

Chasing comets on a bicycle quest,
Wobbling under questions—who'd want to rest?
With each cosmic pedal, a new thought appears,
What if constellations are just cosmic cheers?

Fragments of Wonder in the Milky Way

Galaxies twirl like cotton candy skies,
Sprinkled with starlight and funny goodbyes.
Meteor showers drop jokes like confetti,
Floating through space, we're all a bit petty.

Colliding planets with curious charms,
Each bump a riddle, how do we disarm?
Alien whispers tease us with play,
What's behind Pluto's icy array?

Saucers of laughter soar high and wide,
Chasing the comets on a whimsy ride.
Perhaps the answer lies in a dance,
To question with joy, to joke and to prance!

With every star blink, we giggle at fate,
Are planets just marbles we roll, animate?
Fragments of wonder, we piece them in sight,
Searching for secrets beneath the starlight!

The Tides of Cosmic Curiosity

Waves of wonder crash on sandy shores,
With each tiny shell, the ocean explores.
What secrets do tides cradle in their wave?
Curious minds digging, bold and brave!

Surfboards of questions ride under the sun,
As we ponder if there's an end to the fun?
Splashing through answers, like kids on a spree,
Why does the moon care where the ocean will be?

Seashells echo with giggles from afar,
What if the sands were the first avatars?
The shoreline teases with each gentle sway,
Whispering questions that lead us astray.

In this cosmic sea, we paddle so free,
In the midst of the waves, curious as can be.
With laughter as our compass, let's set sail wide,
Together we'll ride on this cosmic tide!

Constellations of Curiosity

Stars are winking in delight,
What's up there, out of sight?
Aliens peek from their craft,
Laughing at our cosmic graft.

Planets spin with playful grace,
Do they hide a funny face?
Black holes joke with a big grin,
Where do lost socks always begin?

Galaxies swirl, a dizzy show,
Are there space cows, we don't know?
Asteroids dance, twirling in glee,
Is that a UFO or just me?

Wonder fuels this curious quest,
While we laugh, the stars jest.
In the dark, we ponder on,
At least my jokes are never gone!

Nebulae of Not Knowing

Colorful clouds in the night sky,
Are they candy, oh my, oh my?
Each swirl holds a brand new chance,
To catch a glimpse of a cosmic dance.

Whispers of stars, secrets untold,
Do they giggle, kind and bold?
Astrophysicists scratch their heads,
While comets zoom overhead like sleds.

Gaseous tales in cosmic hues,
Are they hiding space-time blues?
Between the questions, darkness reigns,
But we'll punchline through the cosmic chains.

Every twinkle, a riddle, a jest,
Why is gravity such a pest?
A dance of light, a few chuckles,
In nebulae, our humor snuggles!

Astronomical Whys

What makes a shooting star go zing?
Is it a firework or a cosmic fling?
With every blink, a wish unfolds,
Just like grandpa's tales retold.

Why do comets have such long tails?
Do they carry secrets or just tales?
Could Jupiter be a party man?
Or is it just a gassy fan?

Questions circle like asteroids,
Are they pesky or pure joys?
We ponder, laugh, give a shout,
While Saturn spins without a doubt.

Oh, the whys are a playful crew,
Laughing at me and you too!
In the cosmos, the winks flow wide,
The mysteries tickle our cosmic pride!

Light Years of Wonder

In the void, how far is too far?
Can we high-five a passing star?
Distance might make the heart grow fonder,
Or just leave us here to ponder.

How many light years to a giggle?
Is a neutron star just a wiggle?
Shooting stars make wishes bright,
Do they ever wish on their own flight?

Time travelers with silly hats,
Zooming past with laughs and chats,
We stand below, eyes up wide,
Chasing dreams on the cosmic ride.

In this vast and quirky maze,
Each question sparks a wild craze.
Oh, to bask in celestial fun,
Under the whims of a blazing sun!

Cosmic Queries

Why do aliens hide in their craft?
Do they laugh at our Earthly gaffs?
Can they see us stumbling around?
Or are we just noise, moths to the sound?

Does Pluto feel lonely out there?
Or dream of a time when it was fair?
Do black holes play games with our minds?
Or just hoard all the secrets they find?

Are stars really just holes in a sheet?
Or tiny points where aliens tweet?
Do comets have tails just for the show?
Or do they have places to go?

If the moon has a view so divine,
Why does it never send us a sign?
Is the sky just one big cosmic joke?
Or are we the punchline, tethered and broke?

Stars Hanging in Suspense

Why do stars twinkle with such delight?
Are they sharing gossip late at night?
Do they roll their eyes when we wish on them?
Or snicker at dreams, like a cosmic gem?

Is there life on those lonely moons?
Do they sing their own celestial tunes?
Could they send us a postcard or two?
With a smiley face, perhaps, who knew?

Do meteor showers fight for a crown?
Or just fall to Earth, feeling let down?
Are those shooting stars fleeing the scene?
Or are they just crash-test dummies of dreams?

What's with the black holes, all dark and sly?
Do they laugh when we try to reach the sky?
Do they have snacks for the stardust we send?
Or just hoard our secrets to the very end?

Whispers of Infinite Enigma

In a cosmos vast, do thoughts collide?
Do galaxies giggle when we can't decide?
Are quasars just shy, hiding their light?
Or rendering us puzzled, lost in the night?

When the moon pulls tides, does it grimace?
Or dance with glee in its silvered grace?
Are planets envious of our small blue ball?
Or just shaking their heads at our rise and fall?

Is time a friend, or just a wild tease?
Ticking away with abundant ease?
Do comets laugh at their fleeting speed?
While we search for answers we still can't heed?

When telescopes squint at the deep, dark sky,
What secrets are hushed behind each sigh?
Could wormholes be pathways to endless fun?
Or are they just napping, 'til we're done?

Celestial Curiosities

Do shooting stars wish for a day off?
Or are they all saying, 'This is tough'?
Is Saturn just showing off its rings?
Or laughing at Earth and all its flings?

Do we really understand the great void?
Or just choose to leave it all devoid?
Galaxies spinning in cosmic dance,
While we're left to ponder, in a trance?

Do supernovae throw a wild bash?
With confetti stardust, and a loud crash?
Are we just a soap opera on display?
In the grand theater of space's ballet?

When meteorites hit with a boom,
Do they laugh and say, 'Oops, made a room!'?
Can we decipher what's written in light?
Or are the stars just playing us right?

Wandering Through Cosmic Ambivalence

In the vastness, I trip and fall,
Stars chuckle, they're having a ball.
Planets wobble with a wink so sly,
Even black holes need a reason why.

Aliens giggle at our little plight,
While we ponder day and night.
Are we here or just a prank?
Floating in space, all the stars blank.

Galaxies spin like a wild dance,
Making sense is just a chance.
Can I order takeout from Mars?
Or is that just a bunch of stars?

Gravity's pulling, can't break free,
Maybe it's just a cosmic spree.
Is life a jest, or am I lost?
Searching for meaning at such a cost?

The Infinity of What-Ifs

What if time is just a big joke?
Tick tock laughs, while I try to poke.
Maybe yesterday's just a quirk,
A splash in space where thoughts lurk.

What if aliens are watching us eat?
Grabbing popcorn from their plush seat.
Do they giggle at our silly ways?
Juggling planets in cosmic plays?

What if all our dreams are real?
Floating thoughts, like a surreal meal.
Fried moons and baked suns on a plate,
Mmm, space cuisine can't wait!

What if the big bang was a big sneeze?
Creating worlds with cosmic ease.
Oh, what if and maybes rain,
Swirling laughter in a cosmic train?

Nebulae of Curiosity

In the depths of a stellar haze,
I ask questions for days and days.
Are there socks lost in black holes?
Or do galaxies play silly rolls?

Clouds of gas dance in bright colors,
Maybe they're having cosmic slumbers.
Do they wake up with a 'what's next?'
Juggling stardust, feeling perplexed?

Comets speed by with a whoosh and zoom,
Waving at me from their icy tomb.
Are they late for an important call?
Or do they just love to break the wall?

Curiosity spins like a wild kite,
Chasing stars into the night.
Who knows what's out there, oh dear friend?
Just giggle on this quest, it never ends.

The Silent Search for Meaning

I ponder silence in empty space,
Where humor hides with a smiling face.
Stars just wink, as if to tease,
Waiting for answers with cosmic ease.

Asteroids tumble without a care,
While comets whistle through the air.
Is there purpose in their groove?
Or just a party, smoothing their move?

As I drift through the cosmic sea,
I wonder if there's a recipe.
A dash of humor, a pinch of truth,
Stirred with wisdom from eternal youth.

Maybe meaning's a silly dance,
With every question, we take a chance.
Floating through stars, so bright and bold,
In this riddle, laughter's gold.

Questions Adrift in Time

Why is a clock always tick-tocking?
Do fish ever stop and do some talking?
Is coffee the secret to flying high?
And why do donuts never seem to die?

If socks go missing, where do they hide?
Is there a sock thief with nothing to bide?
Do cats think we're all their guards on call?
And who left that banana peel in the hall?

Can one ever truly outrun their thoughts?
Or does the fridge whisper about midnight spots?
If we are the stars, should we shine and twirl?
And do squirrels debate over acorns and pearls?

So many puzzles that twist and bend,
As laughter drips from each curious end.
Let's sip some tea and munch on some bread,
While we ponder the things that swirl in our head.

Constellation of Queries

Do aliens watch us from reliable views?
Selling popcorn while we sing the blues?
What if the stars just want to dance?
And the moon is a guy in a white romance?

When did time start losing its grip?
Or was it just stealing our lunch on a trip?
Are there crickets in space playing the flute?
And do they have parties on asteroids, cute?

If rain is just sky's way of a shower,
Could it be Sunny's turn to feel the power?
Is every comets' tail a sign of a show?
Or just rock confetti from long ago?

Inside this cosmic riddle, we must tread,
With giggles and ponderings filling our head.
So let's laugh at the stars, and chat with the sun,
While we figure this puzzle, haha, it's fun!

The Power of a Luminous Question

Is moon cheese the reason we dream at night?
Or do we just snack on cosmic starlight?
What if every twinkle is a giggle in space?
And the planets are playing a wild little chase?

Why do ducks waddle in their own parade?
Are they the stars of a quacking charade?
If shadows were friends, would they share a drink?
And do they talk secrets? Just stop and think!

Could clouds be pillows that drift in the blue?
While rainbows are secret clubs for the few?
What's really a comet's best-kept delight?
Maybe just cookies baked in the night!

With each silly query, we launch and we spin,
As the magic of wondering ignites from within.
So dance to your questions, let giggles bloom wide,
In this galaxy's riddle, let's savor the ride!

Nebula of Mysteries

Where do all the lost umbrellas reside?
Do rainbows collect them; is that where they hide?
What if the stars are just tipsy and bright?
Creating a party, orbiting light?

Is every hiccup a glitch in the plan?
Or just the universe shaking its can?
Could grass really be the universe's hair?
And does it get tangled if we don't care?

Do clouds discuss politics with the breeze?
Or giggle at shadows, on their knees?
What if the wind is just laughter on roll?
Or do it's whispers always take a toll?

In this nebula of wondrous delight,
Each question a comet, soaring in flight.
So let's chase the whims of this glorious spree,
'Til laughter and mysteries set us all free!

Labyrinth of Cosmological Wonders

Why do stars twinkle like they know the score?
Is it a cosmic joke, a galactic lore?
Planets spin madly, round and round they race,
While comets just giggle, 'We're lost in space!'

What's the sound of a black hole when it sneezes?
A silence so loud, it brings us to pieces.
Wormholes are portals, but where do they lead?
To candy-filled worlds where all answers are freed!

Aliens watch us with popcorn in hand,
Laughing at questions, our thoughts so unmanned.
Do they get lost in their own space-time fuss?
Or maybe they ponder, 'Why all this fuss?'

In the void, where reasons confuse like a riddle,
Each answer we seek just strums on a fiddle.
So let's grab our telescopes and dance in delight,
For every big question may just be a flight!

Questions That Dance Among the Stars

Why do galaxies twirl with such flair and grace?
Are they just showing off, racing through space?
Every stellar jiggle makes us wonder and grin,
Like cosmic performers, they put on a spin!

Are meteors just space rocks having a blast?
Blasting through atmosphere, oh what a fast!
Do they wish to be stars, or just want to play?
While dust bunnies giggle and float on their way.

What if shooting stars are just playful kids?
Sliding down rainbows, through loops and through grids?
Each question a tickle that tickles our minds,
In this vast cosmic playground, fun answers we find!

So here's to the queries that whirl through our heads,
To philosophical thoughts that dance in our beds.
Life's one big question, a curious spree,
Let's laugh at the puzzles, come dance with me!

The Astral Search for Answers

In the depths of the night, we gaze at the skies,
Shooting wishes at stars, asking who, what, and why.
Do planets have secrets they keep up their sleeves?
Or just play hide and seek, causing us to believe?

What's a lightyear, really? Is it just a prank?
A light-speed race with a mysterious flank?
Does space have a license for traveling quick?
Or is it just cruising on a silly cosmic trick?

Each spiral and cluster holds stories untold,
Whispers of stardust in patterns of gold.
As we scribble our memos on interstellar pads,
We're left with the giggles of cosmic nomads.

So here's to the mysteries that swirl in the void,
To the jests of the cosmos—oh what a joy!
For in all of these queries, both wild and profound,
There's laughter and wonder, where answers abound!

Inquiries Adrift in Space

Sailing through starlight on a whimsical ship,
Where questions are treasures, let's take a trip!
Are UFOs just tourists, with maps turned around?
Or aliens saying, 'This world's pretty sound!'

Why do we ponder what's up in the skies?
Are there intergalactic pie-eating highs?
Floating with laughter, we drift on a quest,
With comets as crew, we'll give it our best!

What if black holes are just really big drains?
Sucking up all of our curious gains?
And gravity's just that mysterious force,
That keeps all our dreams on a wild, crazy course!

Let's toast to the wonders and quirks of our fate,
For every big question should never be late.
With humor and joy, let's explore the unknown,
Inquiries adrift, we're never alone!

The Unfathomable Depths

In the vastness where stars play,
Questions linger in a cosmic ballet.
Aliens giggle, they make a fuss,
Why are we here? They ponder, discuss.

Black holes peek and ask for snacks,
While planets spin and take their laps.
Gravity winks, what a silly chap,
Is it all just one giant map?

Comets zoom with cheesy grins,
Slipping through light, chasing their sins.
Asteroids roll like clumsy friends,
In this comedy, the fun never ends.

So, cocktails of gases are brewed with flair,
Nebulae dance like they just don't care.
In the cosmic circus, one secret holds tight,
Laughter echoes through the endless night.

Looking Up: The Quest for Understanding

Gazing upward with a puzzled frown,
Questions swirl like leaves in a town.
Stars wink down, are they in on the joke?
Or just distant lights, having a poke?

Planets whirl in their merry dance,
Do they giggle, or are they in a trance?
Saturn's rings spin around just for fun,
While Pluto hides, saying 'I'm done!'

Telescopes searching for answers with might,
But all they find is a twinkling light.
Scientists scratch their heads with disbelief,
Could it all just be a cosmic leaf?

In the end, what a laugh we share,
Chasing answers through the cosmic air.
With every riddle, we learn to bet,
In this grand game, we're not done yet!

Cosmic Clues Hidden in Time

Time ticks on in this stellar race,
Is it a rabbit or just space's embrace?
Galaxies prance with their mysteries tight,
Like boxers playfully jabbing mid-fight.

Wormholes grin like aged old men,
Time-traveling jokes never end, just begin.
Dimensions wiggle and ask, 'What's the deal?'
Lost in the laughter, we spin this wheel.

Clocks tick backwards, what a funny sight,
While photons tease, saying, 'Catch me if you might!'
The past waves hello, the future says bye,
In this zany dance, who knows, oh my!

Yet among the jokes lies logic's thin thread,
Each peek into the unknown slaps doubt in the head.
In this cosmic riddle, we play and pretend,
That answers await just 'round the next bend.

When Stars Pause to Ask

Stars twinkle, saying, 'What brings you here?'
A cosmic comedy, they hold dear.
Planets giggle, orbiting in track,
While comets shout, 'Don't look back!'

Shooting stars throw wishes with glee,
Is that a dream, or just fantasy?
They slip through the night, blazing bright,
As we ponder life, wrapped tight in delight.

Constellations play connect-the-dots,
Crafting stories, maybe silly plots.
Orion grins, with belt held high,
While the Big Dipper spills tea from the sky.

So here's to questions, both big and small,
In this cosmic circus, there's room for all.
With laughter and wonder, we travel afar,
In the grand mystery, we're all just bizarre.

Dreams Suspended in Galactic Wonder

Stars twinkle, asking why,
Planets spin and laugh nearby.
Comets zoom with grins so wide,
While black holes just want to hide.

Wormholes bend like silly straws,
Aliens cheer with goofy paws.
Asteroids play a game of catch,
In cosmic fields, they find their match.

Nebulas swirl in colors bright,
Painting questions in the night.
While moons tease with a cheeky wink,
And galaxies form a group to think.

In this vast, whimsical dance,
Every star gets a funny chance.
So let's chase stars, don't be shy,
In this playground, oh my, oh my!

Question Marks Breathing in Space

Black holes puff like cosmic steam,
Spinning tales, or so it seems.
With every twirl, they bring delight,
And stars flash silly smiles at night.

Planets wobble, trying to flex,
Polishing their odd syntax.
Saturn's rings just want to race,
While Mercury can't find its place.

Floating thoughts in zero-grav,
Making jokes in cosmic lab.
Comets burst like laughter's song,
In this outer space so wrong!

So raise a glass to cosmic quirks,
The universe's silly works.
In every question lies a jest,
Wonders swirling, never rest!

Cosmic Curiosities

Stars all have their secrets kept,
While black holes giggle, and asteroids crept.
Saturn spins in playful jest,
Juggling moons, like it's the best.

Galaxies whirl in a whimsical dance,
Planets prance in a merry trance.
Nebulas puff out cotton-candy,
While comets fly by all so dandy.

Meteors race with a wink and nod,
Wondering who created this odd facade.
Space is chaos, messy and fun,
As each star shines brighter than the sun.

So let's ponder in laughter and cheer,
What makes this cosmos tick, my dear?
For in every twinkle and cosmic spark,
Lies the fun in questions, never stark!

Stellar Enigmas

Twinkling lights with sneaky glee,
Hidden jokes for us to see.
A galaxy laughs in shades of blue,
While moons play peek-a-boo, it's true!

Mars grumbles, feeling quite red,
Secrets buzzing in its head.
Venus smirks, it knows the game,
Playing coy, it's never lame.

Every supernova shines so bright,
Exploding laughter in the night.
As comets giggle and glide with flair,
Each mystery floats in cosmic air.

So let's explore this funny phase,
Chasing questions in endless maze.
With each riddle lighting our way,
We find the joy in every sway!

Celestial Quandaries

In the night sky, stars play hide and seek,
Planets spin tales, oh what a cheek!
Comets race by, they wave as they pass,
Leaving us wonder if they're made of glass.

Why does Saturn wear rings so grand?
Is it a fashion choice or an alien band?
Black holes are just shy, pulling us near,
Whispering secrets we're too scared to hear.

Uranus just laughs, it rolls on its side,
While Mars flexes arms he can't seem to hide.
Maybe it's all one big cosmic joke,
Witty aliens, laughing at the folks they invoke.

Nebulae of Wonder

In a cloud of gas, colors swirl and play,
Like a cosmic painter in disarray.
Why do stars twinkle, do they need a nap?
Or are they just styling in a cosmic cap?

The milky way stretches, a ribbon of light,
But does it get tangled on a cloudy night?
Distant galaxies wink, don't they get tired?
Or is it our eyes that have just expired?

Supernovas pop like fireworks bright,
While aliens giggle at the human plight.
Counting the stars? Oh what a mess!
They're all just hiding in cosmic dress!

Dark Matter Mystique

In shadows, yes, the answers might dwell,
But they giggle and scoot, oh can't you tell?
What's the matter with dark, can't it shine?
Is it just bashful or sipping on wine?

Is gravity a prank just pulling our strings?
Making us ponder all these strange things?
Invisible forces at play, pulling tight,
While we just scratch our heads in the night.

Quasars are chaos, like a cosmic show,
They flicker and flap, then put on a glow.
What's the recipe for space that we see?
A pinch of wonder, and a dash of glee?

Astrological Ambiguities

Stars up above, they giggle in line,
Reading our fates through an astrological sign.
Mercury's in retrograde, oh what a fuss,
Do planets get gossipy, just like us?

Gemini twins are just double the fun,
But Virgos keep lists; how boring, oh pun!
Taurus loves snacks, while Leos take charge,
Do planets hold meetings, oh my, it's large!

Our zodiac sketches, a cosmic caricature,
Maybe our horoscopes are meant to lure.
So let's laugh at the stars, their celestial play,
As they dance and they twirl, our fears lead astray!

Celestial Whimsy

Stars giggle in the night,
Planets play hide and seek,
Jupiter whispers secrets,
While Saturn gives a cheeky peek.

Asteroids throw confetti,
Comets dance in a line,
Black holes sip on lemonade,
As constellations intertwine.

Galaxies wear funny hats,
Twinkling with a silly flair,
Wormholes tie their shoelaces,
With laughter in the cosmic air.

Why does Mars have all the fun?
Venus frowns and shakes her head,
While Earth is planting daisies,
In this garden of what's ahead.

A Tapestry of Questions

Why do meteors cry at night?
Perhaps they miss their starry friends,
Chasing comets in the light,
Where the strangeness never ends.

Aliens debate about snacks,
Popcorn or chocolate, which is best?
They zoom and zerk in their tracks,
On quests for a cosmic feast quest.

Nebulas weave stories bright,
Of cosmic giggles and glee,
Each braid a wondering sight,
Tickling the vast galaxy.

Saturn's rings hold a dance,
Inviting all stars to join,
Spinning in a joyful trance,
On a quest for the next big coin.

Galactical Question Marks

What if black holes misplace things?
And forgot their cosmic shoes?
Rings of Saturn play with slings,
Creating a universe of blues.

Pulsars tick-tock like grand clocks,
What are they counting, and why?
Do they ponder if time unlocks,
Mysteries that float on by?

Quasars laugh in bursts of light,
Tickling dark matter's cheek,
With cosmic whispers soft and bright,
While exploring what they seek.

Cosmic dust sneezes with flair,
Scattering stars in a show,
Who knew the sky could care,
With questions they love to throw!

Skydancers of Inquiry

Shooting stars serve funny lines,
As they twirl across the dusk,
Do they know about our signs?
Or are they dancing just for husk?

Galaxies do a waltz,
In pairs of spirals we see,
Who steps on whose faults?
Spinning forever, so free.

Alien jokes in the night,
Crackling through the cosmic waves,
Do they ponder our delight,
Or simply laugh as they rave?

Sidereal mysteries abound,
As the universe spins and twirls,
With laughter, joy is found,
In a realm where magic unfurls.

Questions in the Cosmos

Why do stars twinkle in the night?
Are they just playing hide and seek with light?
Do aliens watch us while we snore?
Or are they debating who made the best s'more?

If time is money, where's my change?
Do black holes switch it up, feeling strange?
Do planets ever feel a bit shy?
Or just spin around, not caring why?

When comets rush by like they own the place,
Do they wave hello or just quicken their pace?
Is Jupiter just a giant gas bag?
Or a party planet where no one can lag?

And what about gravity, that trusty friend?
Does it pull you close, or just pretend?
Are we all just dots on a cosmic pinball?
Waiting for someone to hit the next call?

Beyond the Horizon of Thought

If I could ask a quasar a question so bold,
Would it laugh at my woes or just get cold?
Do black holes eat socks when I'm not aware?
Is every lost sock a space-time affair?

What makes a meteor shower so bright?
Is it just stars having a pillow fight?
Do we think too much about what's up there?
While aliens giggle and just don't care?

Do nebulae gossip about their past blunders?
Do galaxies whisper while the earth just wonders?
If I traveled light-years to meet a star,
Would it question my sense, or laugh from afar?

And if time travel's real, let's make a pact,
To visit the future and see what we lacked.
But what if I saw my own self again?
Would I high-five or let out a groan of, "When?"

Mysteries in the Milky Way

In the Milky Way, do chocolates float?
Or is it just candy that I've thought up? (No joke!)
Do shooting stars wish they had more flair?
Or just wish for someone to care, or a chair?

Is Mars just waiting for its big debut?
Dressed in red, trying to find a crew?
Does Venus laugh at our earthly plight?
Or just sit and sip cosmic tea at night?

What's the deal with time that ticks away?
Does it join the stars in some grand ballet?
If I catch a wormhole for a quick ride,
Will it take me to fun, or far and wide?

Do aliens skydive off comets with glee?
While sipping on lattes, just you and me?
On a quest for answers, what a wild ride!
In the game of inquiry, there's no need to hide!

The Void of Inquiry

In the void of space, is there a big laugh?
Do asteroids chuckle at our math?
Is every black hole a party's end?
Or a cosmic note played, just to send?

When meteors zoom and crash down in spree,
Do they scream, "Watch out, it's not just me?"
Or do they giggle thinking it's a joke?
While we run for cover, oh, what a poke!

Do solar flares flare up in pure jest?
While planets sit back, wearing their best?
Is Pluto still sulking, or having fun?
Sipping space drinks, plotting how to run?

Maybe the cosmos is a game we all play,
With questions and riddles from night until day.
Let's grab a telescope, look up and see,
In this grand scheme, just let it be free!

Elements of the Unknown

What if atoms play hide and seek,
And bosons are the ones that sneak?
Each black hole's just a curious cat,
Swatting at stardust, imagine that!

Quarks dance like leaves in the breeze,
While neutrinos do as they please.
Is the Higgs boson just a rumor?
Or a lost sock's charming tailor?

In every spark, a mystery spins,
Like socks lost, or where the fun begins.
Behind every particle, a cheeky grin,
As the cosmos spins, we all join in!

So raise a toast to physics' quirks,
To bubbles popping and witty jerks.
In a world adrift, with laughter stored,
Who's got the answers? The galaxies snored!

The Language of Stars

Stars gossip in twinkling light,
Trading secrets deep in the night.
A comet winks with a trail of glee,
"Catch me if you can!" it shouts with spree!

Constellations do a silly dance,
Dressed in diamonds, they take a chance.
What if Orion just lost his belt?
And Venus dropped a cupcake, how we felt!

The Milky Way offers cosmic bread,
Made of starlight and dreams in our head.
As meteor showers bless the sky,
We laugh and wonder, oh me, oh my!

So gather 'round for tales so bold,
Of galaxies spun like stories told.
In this cosmic joke, we'll never fail,
To find delight in every tale!

Enigma in Every Eclipse

When shadows nibble on the sun,
We giggle because it's all in fun.
"Peek-a-boo!" cries the moon so sly,
As we blink and wonder, "Oh my, oh my!"

A solar party with lights turned down,
Is it a crown or a cosmic frown?
While planets juggle in the dark,
Eclipses create quite the spark!

Like kids on a playground at dusk,
The sun and moon, in a game of trust.
What's behind that curtain of night?
A wink from the cosmos? What a delight!

So tip your hat to lunar fun,
In this grand circus, all can run.
In shadows and light, we find our cheer,
As every eclipse brings laughter near!

Celestial Paradoxes

What if the planets all play chess,
And gravity just loves to impress?
With pawns made of comets flying high,
And the king is a star who just won't die!

Neptune laughs at Saturn's rings,
While several moons dance and sing.
Are black holes just cosmic vacuums?
Sucking in dreams, while avoiding gloom?

If time travels sideways, does it giggle?
Or dance like a worm with a fun wiggle?
With every paradox, the jokes grow tall,
Are we all part of one big comedy hall?

So let's toast to the quirks all around,
In this stellar carnival, joy is found.
With laughter echoing from star to star,
We're all just creatures under a twinkling bazaar!

Questions Wrapped in Stardust

What if stars are just shy sparks,
Dancing around in cosmic parks?
Are aliens lost in their own ways,
Or just hiding during our busy days?

Why do planets spin in such a rush,
While moons just sit and nonchalantly hush?
Is space a joke, a cosmic prank,
Or are we the punchline to a galactic prank?

Space: An Endless Inquiry

Why does gravity keep us down?
Is it just to stop us spinning 'round?
Do asteroids dream of a gentle touch,
Or fear the vacuum far too much?

Could black holes be cosmic vacuums,
Sucking away all our youthful blooms?
If light can bend, why can't we?
In this expanse, who's the biggest bee?

Comets of Contemplation

Are comets just cosmic ice cream trucks,
Delivering flavors that run amok?
Why do they leave a glowing tail,
Like they're speeding past on a grand highway trail?

Is there a space race we don't know?
Where Martians cheer as comets flow?
When stars collide, do they shake hands?
Or is it just chaos in distant lands?

The Sky is a Question

If clouds have feelings, what do they think?
Do they ever worry they'll spill their ink?
Is the sun a jester with a fiery grin,
Playing peek-a-boo as daylight begins?

When lightning strikes, does it yell surprise?
Are stars just winks in the cosmic skies?
In this grand stage of endless quests,
Are we just guests, or part of the jest?

The Light of Inquiry

In the vastness, we ponder, oh so bright,
Questions dance like stars, out of sight.
What's that up there? Is it cheese, or pie?
Aliens giggling, swirling by!

With telescopes peering into the night,
Searching for answers, we squint with delight.
Do black holes have parties? Is space full of glee?
Or just empty wonders, for you and for me?

Asteroids bounce like kids in a game,
While comets zoom past, none feel the same.
Are we just a joke in a galactic jest?
Laughing at questions, is curiosity best?

So let's raise a laugh, and give it a whirl,
Every new thought is a twirl and a swirl.
In this cosmic circus, let's join in the fun,
With giggles and queries, there's always more to run!

Answers Written in Starlight

In constellations, answers hide and seek,
Questions like fireflies, twinkle and peek.
Is Jupiter a giant with a wig so grand?
Or just a planet with tales unplanned?

Nebulas giggle, with colors so bright,
Each spark is a riddle, soaring through night.
Could Saturn's rings be a hula hoop game?
Or simply a fashion from a cosmic fame?

The Milky Way winks, hints at a clue,
What if the planets all dance like a crew?
If meteors cry, do they laugh in the end?
Just trying to figure out how to spend!

So up in the sky, let's question the lore,
With laughter and wonder, there's always more.
In this galaxy's tale, let joy take its flight,
For answers are games, and starlight is bright!

Echoes in the Cosmic Silence

In silence so loud, where echoes collide,
Questions emerge, like a cosmic tide.
Do voids have whispers, or is it just sound?
Are black holes a portal for lost thoughts unbound?

Quasars hum tunes from eons ago,
Tickling our brains with a cosmic flow.
If time is a river, do clocks ever sleep?
Or tick-le the stars in a dance, wide and deep?

Galaxies wobble in a clumsy spin,
What if they trip? Would they laugh or just grin?
With laughter so booming, let's laugh with the night,
For in this still space, there's joy in the flight!

Echoes of questions bounce far and near,
Each twinkling star brings us giggles to cheer.
So ponder with mirth in this silent delight,
In cosmic confusion, let's dance with our light!

Orbiting Uncertainty

Around and around, we spin with a grin,
In orbit of questions, where do we begin?
Are planets just friends having parties galore?
Or ships lost in space, forever to explore?

Asteroids wobble, like toys in a box,
While comets dash by, ticking cosmic clocks.
Do stars get together for chat sessions late?
Or is it just silence, their favorite fate?

Gravity's pull is a friendly embrace,
Is it a dance-off in this vast open space?
We'll twirl and we'll giggle, while missing the aim,
At least in uncertainty, we can all share a name!

So join in the fun, don your astronaut suit,
In this wild cosmic ride, never be mute.
With laughter and queries, we'll hang on so tight,
Orbiting uncertainty feels just so right!

Chasing the Infinite Question

In the cosmos, I wander, oh what a sight,
Planets giggle, stars twinkle in delight.
A galaxy of puzzles, who swiped the cheese?
Asteroids chuckle as we float with ease.

Do aliens ponder like humans do?
Or sip their drinks while watching us too?
The black holes whisper secrets untold,
As comets race by, taunting and bold.

What if our thoughts are mere echoes here?
Or time's just a joke that we pretend to clear?
A cosmic riddle wrapped in dark lace,
Where confusion dances in endless space.

Each question I ask gives rise to more,
The stars just wink from their celestial floor.
So here I drift with a smile on my face,
Chasing the infinite with curious grace.

Stars and Silence: A Conversation

Two stars are chatting in the quiet night,
One says, "What's new? Did you see that light?"
The other replies, with a twinkle of glee,
"Solving our mysteries is harder than we see!"

They scratch their heads, as galaxies swirl,
Discussing if gravity's just a lost pearl.
"Is space a big joke?" one brave star asked,
While others just giggled at the questions they masked.

"What's at the end? A giant door?
Or merely more questions for us to explore?"
Between the winks, laughter bounces through,
A celestial chat filled with cosmic brew.

As dawn knocks softly, the chatter subsides,
They fade into sunlight, but friendship abides.
Their cosmic banter, a curious game,
Forever tied in the universe's name.

What Lies Beyond the Veil

Behind the curtain where light disappears,
Do martians play chess while sipping on beers?
An astronaut wonders, peeking through time,
Can aliens laugh? Or is it a crime?

As thoughts drift like ships on a starry sea,
What if pink unicorns giggle with glee?
The void rolls its eyes at the quirky parade,
While comets throw confetti, unafraid.

Each mystery wrapped in a riddle so bold,
Could theories be jokes that our minds have told?
What lies beyond is a whimsical tease,
With quantum mischief blowing in the breeze.

Yet here we stand, unfazed by the quest,
Embracing the questions we love the best.
In every "why" and "how," there's a twist,
To probe the unknown, you simply can't resist.

Dreaming in Stardust

In my dreams, I'm sailing a cosmic ship,
Through stardust and questions, I take a trip.
Chasing light beams like a child with a kite,
Wishing for answers in the endless night.

Galaxies giggle, stars blink with delight,
As I ask them things about their weird plight.
"Do you snicker at Earth and all of its fuss?"
A supernova winks, like "Why bother, just trust!"

Galactic wisdom floats in the air,
Like cotton candy spun bright and rare.
What if the answers are lost in a rhyme?
A dance of the cosmos transcending time.

So, I'll float on this dream, a question in tow,
Laughing with wonders that shimmer and glow.
For beneath every query, a joke can be found,
In a universe where laughter knows no bounds.

www.ingramcontent.com/pod-product-compliance
Lightning Source LLC
Chambersburg PA
CBHW072214070526
44585CB00015B/1334